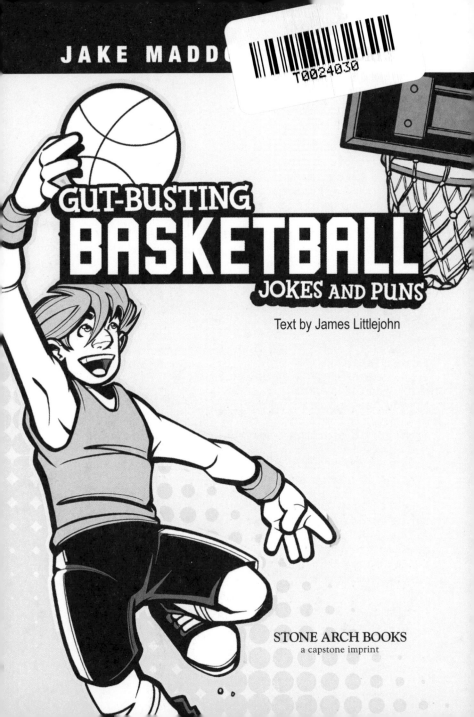

JAKE MADD

GUT-BUSTING
BASKETBALL
JOKES AND PUNS

Text by James Littlejohn

STONE ARCH BOOKS
a capstone imprint

Published by Stone Arch Books,
an imprint of Capstone.
1710 Roe Crest Drive
North Mankato, Minnesota 56003
capstonepub.com

Library of Congress Cataloging-in-Publication Data
is available on the Library of Congress website.
ISBN: 9781669074854 (library binding)
ISBN: 9781669074892 (paperback)
ISBN: 9781669075127 (ebook PDF)

Summary: If you love basketball—and a good laugh—
then this is the book for you! With more than 170
hilarious jokes, riddles, and funny puns, you and
your friends will be laughing to the last page!

Editor: Aaron Sautter
Designer: Jaime Willems
Production Specialist:
Whitney Schaefer
Design Elements: Nana Chen,
Shutterstock/Vector FX

Printed and bound in China. PO 5827

TABLE OF CONTENTS

Why can't you play basketball with a phone?

It'd be a moving screen.

What's a referee's least favorite kind of shoes?

Flip *flop*s.

Why'd the cheapskate keep committing fouls?

He loved *free* throws.

What did the basketball player do before blowing out the candles on her cake?

She made a *swish*!

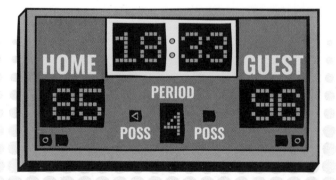

What did the referee say to the basketball player who started an argument?

"Do you have a *point* to make?"

Why'd the ref blow her whistle at the airport?

She saw a lot of traveling.

Why didn't anyone take the ref seriously?

He was always making prank calls.

What do you call a referee who won't stop blowing her whistle?

Foul-tempered.

Why don't you want twins on your basketball team?

They'll get called for double dribbling.

How'd the point guard beat his opponent down the court?

He untied the opponent's shoelaces.

What is a game called when nobody scores?

Pointless.

How'd the point guard beat the entire team down the court?

He tied their shoelaces together.

Coach: Hey ref, you need glasses!

Player: So do you—I'm not the ref!

WHY DID THE CHICKEN . . . ?

Why did the chicken cross the court?

To get to the other sideline.

Why did the chicken run across the court?

Because it was a fast break.

Why did the chicken stop running?

It got to the *fowl* line.

What did the announcer say when the chicken made the jump shot?

"It was poultry in motion!"

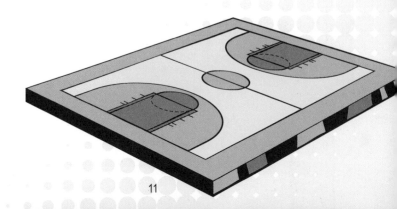

Why did the coach encourage the hen?

He wanted to egg her on.

Why did the ref blow the whistle when he saw a chicken?

Because there was a fowl on the court.

Why'd the chicken get called for a technical?

Because of his fowl language.

Why did the fans cheer?

Because the ref made an *egg*-cellent call.

Why did the crowd get so loud?

They were rooster boosters.

Why did the hen always hit her shots?

She always put her eggs in one basket.

What did the chicken say when it ran into her teammate?

Eggs-cuse me!

Why were fans laughing at the announcer's call?

She was a real comedi-*hen*.

Why did the trainer come onto the court?

Because the chicken needed an *eggs*-ray.

Why did the benchwarmer sketch chickens on the sideline?

She wanted to draw some fowls!

Why did the chicken cross the basketball court?

Better question: Why is there a basketball court in the middle of a chicken farm?

Why wouldn't the guard go on vacation?

Because the coach told her to stop traveling.

Why'd the coach give the player a shoelace?

They were trying to tie up the score!

Why'd the coach make his players wear mittens?

So they'd have a hot hand in the game.

Why'd the coach buy a trampoline?

So the players could work on their bounce passes!

Why'd the coach call 911?

Because the other team was on fire.

What did the genie say after the coach rubbed the lamp?

"I will grant you three *swishes* for the game."

What did the coach say to the genie when she made her wish?

"I *hoop* we get a win!"

What food do coaches hate the most?

Turnovers!

Coach: You have your sneakers on the wrong feet.

Player: But these are the only feet I've got!

What did the coach feed his players so they would try harder?

Hustle sprouts.

GO TEAM

Coach: How'd you get the black eye?

Player: You see that pole under the hoop?

Coach: Yeah.

Player: I didn't.

Player: Hey Coach, think we'll win the championship?

Coach: *Hoop*-fully!

How many coaches does it take to screw in a light bulb?

It doesn't matter. Even if you have 100, they'll just tell *you* how to do it.

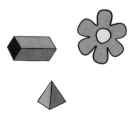

21

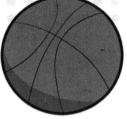

Why did the cashier foul out?

She was always charging.

Why do construction workers make bad shooters?

They're always laying bricks.

Why didn't the farmer play defense on the court?

She was cherry picking.

What is a fisherman's favorite shot?

A hook shot.

What position does an electrician play?

Power forward.

Which area of the court do artists love to play on?

The paint.

When does a janitor start watching the game?

During garbage time.

Why was the baker
so hard to stop?

He was the best at pick-n-*rolls.*

What do you call it
when a baker scores?

A bread basket.

Why'd the police
come to the game?

They heard someone
shot the ball.

Where did the locksmith always want to play?

In the key.

Why did the coach want a carpenter on the team?

They were great at getting boards.

Why didn't anyone want to play with the garbage collector?

Because he was always talking trash.

What kind of doctors do basketball players see?

Hoop-ticians!

Why did the computer programmer get ejected from the game?

He had too many *technical* fouls.

SECTION 5:
HIGH-FLYIN' FUNNIES

What is a basketball player's favorite dessert?

Cookies. Because she loves to dunk them!

Why was the player always knitting?

He wanted to make a jumper.

Why was the fan cheering from the cheap seats?

He loved to watch *free* throws.

How was the basketball feeling after it scored?

Well-rounded.

What do you call a basketball on a plane?

An air ball.

Why did the basketball player have to go to the bank?

Her checks kept bouncing.

What are basketball players called in Hawaii?

Hula-*hoop*-ers!

What do you call a potato watching from the stands?

A spec-*tater*!

Why was the ball hog such a slow driver?

He refused to pass.

Why is basketball the grossest sport?

Because players are always dribbling all over the court.

Why did the players put lucky pennies in their sneakers?

They were *hooper*-stitious.

What's a basketball player's favorite food?

A *jam* sandwich.

What did the player say when the pass went out of bounds?

Alley *"oops!"*

Why did the players bring a heater instead of their uniforms?

They were benchwarmers.

Why did the point guard bring a car into the arena?

She loved to *drive* down the court.

Why was the guard's car such a mess?

She always dribbled as she drove.

Why did the player bring toast to the game?

Because of all the jams!

When is the one time you don't want a point guard to pass?

When he has gas!

What's a basketball player's second-best sport?

Hula *hoop*-ing.

What kind of food did the team order when they were behind?

Thai food.

Why didn't the player get the joke about the bad pass?

It was way over her head.

Why didn't the nose make the team?

Because it didn't get picked!

SECTION 6:
WILD PLAYS

What did the ref do when the elephant charged on the court?

He got out of the way!

Why did the duck take a charge during the game?

To prove she wasn't a chicken.

Why wouldn't the cow take a charge?

It was a *cow*-ard.

Why was the sheep at the basketball game?

She heard the G.O.A.T. was playing.

What do you call a mallard who can make big shots?

A slam duck!

What's the difference between a basketball player and a dog?

One drools while the other dribbles.

How did the birds get ready for the game?

By doing their *worm*-ups.

Why was everyone mad at the pig?

Because it was such a ball hog.

Why did the crowd boo the cat?

Because it coughed up a h-*air*-ball.

What do you call a high-flying sheep?

A *lamb*-dunker.

Did you hear about the bird that never missed a shot?

It was im-*peck*-able.

What do you call a T-Rex that can ball?

A dino-*scorer*!

Why did the coach pick the frog to join the team?

Because he always made his jump shots!

Why did the cat get kicked out of the game?

It was a *cheat*-ah!

Why did the fish stop playing the basketball game?

Because it was afraid of the nets.

How did the seabird break the rules?

It was caught *gull*-tending.

Why did the dog get ejected from the game?

It had too many *flea*-grant fouls.

Did you hear about the lion that tried to play basketball?

It was a total *cat*-astrophe.

Why was everyone cheering the frog?

It was great at making bounce passes.

Why wouldn't the bee watch the end of the game?

It hated buzzer-beaters.

Did you hear about the skunk that tried playing basketball?

It really stunk.

What did they call the hippo that could dunk?

A *hop*-popotamus.

Why did the bird make such a bad coach?

It was always just winging it.

SECTION 7:
SILLY KNOCK-KNOCKERS

Knock-knock.
Who's there?

Ali
Ali who?

**I'm looking for Oop–
have you seen him?**

Knock-knock.
Who's there?

Heckling fan.
Heckling fan—

BOOOOOOOOOO!

Knock-knock.
Who's there?

Instant replay.
Instant replay who?

Knock-knock.

Knock-knock.
Who's there?

Boo.
Boo who?

**Don't cry, it's just a game!
We'll win the next one.**

Knock-knock.
Who's there?

The referee.
The referee who?

Breet! That's a technical foul for questioning an official.

Knock-knock.
Who's there?

Knock-knock.
Who's there?

Knock-knock.
Who's there?

Breet! Delay of game!

Knock-knock.
Who's there?

Timeout!
Timeout who?

Hold on—I'll tell you in 30 seconds.

BIG-MAN LAUGHS

What was the big player's favorite kind of story?

Tall tales.

What did the basketball coach give the waiter?

A tall order.

Why did everyone want to talk to the 7-footer?

He was the *center* of attention.

Why did NASA want to hire the big basketball player?

They were searching for the *center* of the universe.

Why was the center in such a bad mood?

She was bored of getting boards.

Why'd the center play so much Minecraft?

She loved making blocks.

Why couldn't the big center listen to music?

Because he broke all the records.

Why was the basketball player fishing in a cloud?

He was working on his sky hook.

Why can't a guard be 7 feet tall?

Because then they'd be a center.

Why did the 7-foot player bring a turkey to the court?

He wanted to practice "stuffing."

What do you call a 3-foot player?

A baby center.

What do you call a 5-foot player?

A youth center.

What do you call a 6-foot player who used to be a 7-footer?

A senior center.

Where can you trade a 7-foot player?

At the shopping center.

How do you talk to a 7-foot player?

Through the call center.

What do you call a 7-foot player in downtown?

City center.

What do you call a 7-foot player who's volunteering?

Service center.

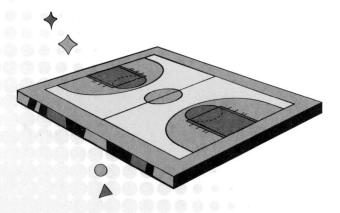

CROSSOVER CRACK-UPS

How do benchwarmers cool off at the game?

They sit near all the fans.

Why was the team sleeping during practice?

They wanted to be like the dream team.

What did the ref say to the team that had no guards?

You're *point*-less.

What's an invisible man's favorite basketball shot?

The fadeaway.

Why did the fan bring his kids' toys to the game?

Because his team needed some blocks.

What do you call a vampire playing basketball?

A *jam*-pire!

Why did the basketball team want a baseball player?

They heard about his grand *slam*.

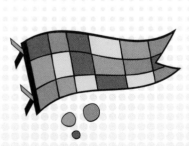

What do you call a basketball game with too many rebounds?

A board game.

What do you call a basketball game with too many replays?

A video game.

What do you call it when rock stars are dunking the ball?

A jam session.

What did the player who couldn't shoot do after getting cut?

He became a bricklayer.

Why did the dog miss the layup?

Its owner told him to lay down.

Why'd the basketball player go to jail?

She stole the ball.

What do you call it when a player hurts their leg when running down the court?

A fast break.

What is a weaver's favorite sport?

Basket-ball.

What do basketball players love to snack on the most?

Swish cheese!

What do you call a basketball player who's always telling jokes?

A *court* jester.

What do you call a basketball player who's faster than a speeding bullet?

Hooper-man!

Where did the basketball-playing twins sleep every night?

In their *dunk* beds.

Why wouldn't the skeleton play basketball?

His heart just wasn't in it.

Can an All-Star player jump higher than Mount Everest?

Definitely! Mountains can't jump!

Why'd the Wizards' coach call a timeout?

So the players could sit down for a spell.

What do you call the Timberwolves when they play the Suns?

Hot dogs.

Why did the Hornets fans think they'd win it all?

They were *bee*-lievers.

How do the Phoenix Mercury decide what play to run?

They planet.

What do you call a Pelicans player who is ejected from the game?

A Pelican't.

Why were the Jazz fans so worried?

The team was in *treble*.

What kind of sneakers do the Grizzlies play in?

They don't. They play *bear*-footed!

What did the prince dream of becoming one day?

One of the Sacramento Kings.

What happened when the Hornets played the Clippers?

They got buzz cuts.

Why couldn't the basketball player sit still?

He was a Pacer.

Which team has the hardest time finding a mascot?

The Raptors. Dinosaurs are extinct.

Did you hear about the basketball fan who was bad at counting?

He rooted for the 75ers!

Why'd the Denver Nuggets have to miss the game?

They caught a gold.

Did you hear about the Timberwolf who swallowed the shot clock?

He got ticks.

Why'd the Seattle Storm player get so embarrassed?

Somebody saw their *thunder*-wear.

Why'd all the lobsters root for the Knicks?

Because they didn't want to be around the Nets.

Did you hear about the Magic's new coach?

He got so mad he pulled his hare out.

Where do the Bucks go to get breakfast?

The local *doe*-nut shop!

How do fans in Miami feel about their team?

It's a love-Heat relationship.

Did you hear about the time lightning struck the Thunder's arena?

It was pretty shocking!

Why are the Bulls the richest basketball team?

Because they charge the most.

Have you ever seen the Hawks mascot swimming in a lake?

They call it the Hawk Ness Monster.

How do players in Houston eat their guacamole?

On a Rocket chip.

Which team did the barber cheer for?

The Los Angeles Clippers.

TELLING FUNNY JOKES!

1. Know your joke.
Be sure you memorize the whole joke before you tell it. Most of us have heard someone start a joke by saying, "Oh, this is SO funny . . ." But then they can't remember part of it. Or they forget the ending, which is the most important part of the joke—the punch line!

2. Speak up.
Don't mumble your words. And don't speak too fast or too slow. Just speak clearly. You don't have to use a strange voice or accent. (Unless that's part of the joke!)

3. Look at your audience.
Good eye contact with your listeners will grab and hold their attention.

4. Don't overthink things.
You don't need to use silly gestures to tell your joke, unless it helps sell the punch line. You can either sit or stand to tell your jokes. Make yourself comfortable. Remember, telling jokes is basically just talking to people to make them laugh.

5. Don't laugh at your own joke.
Sure, comedians sometimes crack up laughing while they're telling a story. And that can be pretty funny by itself. But normally, it's best not to laugh at your own jokes. If you do, you might lose the timing of your joke or mess it up. Let your audience do the laughing. Your job is to be the funny one.

6. Practice your setup.

The setup is the second most important part of a joke. This includes everything you say before getting to the punch line. Be as clear as you can so when you reach the punch line, it makes sense!

7. Get the punch line right.

The punch line is the most important part of the joke. It's the payoff to the main event. A good joke is best if you pause for a second or two before delivering the punch line. That tiny pause will make your audience pay attention, eager to hear what's coming next.

8. Practice, practice, practice.

Practice your routine until you know it by heart. You can also watch other comedians or a comedy show or film. Listen to other people tell a joke. Pay attention to what makes them funny. You can pick up skills by seeing how others get an audience laughing. With enough practice, you'll soon be a great comedian.

9. It's all about the timing.

Learn to get the timing right for the biggest impact. Waiting for the right time and giving that extra pause before the punch line can really zing an audience. But you should also know when NOT to tell a joke. You probably know when your friends like to hear something funny. But when around unfamiliar people, you need to "read the room" first. Are people having a good time? Or is it a more serious event? A joke is funniest when it's told in the right setting.

BASKETBALL TERMS TO KNOW

board (BOHRD)—another name for a rebound

brick (BRIK)—an attempted shot that hits the rim and doesn't go into the basket

center (SEN-tuhr)—a player who is usually the tallest on the team and responsible for getting rebounds and playing defense near the basket

charge (CHARJ)—an offensive foul in which the player with the ball rushes into a defender

cherry pick (CHAIR-ee PIK)—when a player decides to stay near the opponent's goal instead of playing defense in the hope of getting the ball back to score easy points

dunk (DUHNK)—when a player jumps above the rim and puts the ball directly through the hoop with both hands

fadeaway (FAYD-uh-way)—a jump shot taken while jumping backward to create space between the shooter and the defender

fast break (FAST BRAKE)—when a team attempts to advance the ball and score as quickly as possible

forward (FOR-wurd)—a player whose main job is to score points

free throw (FREE THROH)—a free shot taken from the free-throw line after a defender commits a foul against a player

guard (GARD)—a player whose main jobs are to pass the ball, move it down the court, and score points

hook shot (HOOK SHOT)—a shot in which a player swings the ball over their head with one arm to shoot it with a curved motion into the net

jam (JAM)—another name for a dunk

key (KEE)—the area of the court that includes the free-throw line and the circle

rebound (REE-bound)—when a player regains possession of the ball after a missed shot

technical foul (TEK-nuh-kuhl FOUL)—a foul called for unsportsmanlike behavior

travel (TRAV-uhl)—to move more than one foot while holding the basketball or to take three or more steps without dribbling the ball

GLOSSARY

benchwarmer (BENCH-war-muhr)—a reserve player who sits on the bench for most or all of a game

G.O.A.T. (GOHT)—short for the Greatest of All Time

guacamole (gwah-kuh-MOH-lee)—a dip made of mashed avocados mixed with tomato, onion, and seasonings

hare (HAIR)—an animal that looks like a large rabbit with long, strong back legs

treble (TREB-uhl)—a high-pitched or shrill voice, tone, or sound

ABOUT THE AUTHOR

James Littlejohn is a writer, dad, and sports fan. He's played basketball since he was a kid. He also enjoys tennis, soccer, backyard wiffle ball, and just about any board game. He lives with his family and energetic golden retriever in southern California. James is the author of *B is for Baller, S is for Slugger,* and *G is for Golazo* in the ABC to MVP series.

READ THEM ALL!

JAKE MADDOX SPORTS JOKES

GUT-BUSTING
BASKETBALL
JOKES AND PUNS

JAKE MADDOX SPORTS JOKES

HILARIOUS
DANCE, CHEER,
AND **GYMNASTICS**
JOKES AND PUNS

JAKE MADDOX SPORTS JOKES

LAUGH-OUT-LOUD
FOOTBALL
JOKES AND PUNS

JAKE MADDOX SPORTS JOKES

SIDE-SPLITTING
SOCCER
JOKES AND PUNS